Music Education for All

Planning Effective and Inclusive Lessons the UDL Way

SARAH FARD

UNTIL LEARNING HAS NO LIMITS™

For information about special discounts for bulk purchases, please email publishing@cast.org or visit publishing.cast.org

© 2025 CAST, Inc.
All rights reserved.

All rights reserved. No part of this publication may be reproduced, stored in a retrieval system, or transmitted in any form or by any means, electronic, mechanical, photocopying, recording, or otherwise, without the prior permission of the Publisher.

Library of Congress Control Number: 2025936877

ISBN (paperback): 978-1-943085-37-8
ISBN (ebook): 978-1-943085-38-5

Published by:
CAST Professional Publishing
an imprint of CAST, Inc.
Lynnfield, Massachusetts, USA

SKINNY BOOKS® is a registered trademark of CAST, Inc.

Cover and interior design by Happenstance Type-O-Rama
Cover illustration: © iStockPhoto | Murata Yuki

Contents

About the Author

Foreword: My Story

1 The Beginning Is the End 1

2 Engaging Students:
Why Should I Take This Class? 5

3 Represent! What Is Music Literacy? 17

4 How Do We Know They Know? 29

5 Just a Note Before You Go 41

6 Sample Lessons 51

References 81

About the Author

Sarah Fard is a high school music teacher in Massachusetts, where she teaches full inclusion music electives. Over the course of her career she has taught every grade in the public school system, including general music, chorus, band, and the music technology and popular music classes that she teaches now. After earning her bachelor's degree in music education from the University of New Hampshire, Sarah found herself working as a paraprofessional for students with various disabilities. This work set her on a path to seeking greater equity and access for both students and teachers. She completed her master's in music education at Boston University, followed by a graduate certificate in music education and autism at the Boston Conservatory at Berklee College of Music.

In addition to teaching high school music, Sarah is an adjunct professor at the Longy School of Music of Bard College's Master of Music Education program. She is also an active member of the Massachusetts Music Educators Association, serving on the DEIA committee and supporting new performance opportunities for underrepresented students. She is passionate about supporting other teachers in their inclusive efforts, whether it is through workshops, webinars, sharing materials, or one-on-one mentoring with pre-service and first-year teachers. When she is not teaching, she is performing in the New England area.

Foreword: My Story

My first year of teaching was difficult, as it is for many new teachers. I was teaching eighth-grade general music to students who had not had music classes in years. There were no instruments or curriculum. Class sizes were of roughly 35 students each, including a high percentage of English learners and students with special education support needs. Due to staffing shortages, one-on-one support for students with disabilities was nonexistent. With no blueprint, I created a curriculum based on what I thought I should be teaching.

Though I was a jazz guitarist with a background in pop and rock, I had been taught that music education valued Western classical music, with an emphasis on basic reading and writing of staff notation. I struggled through the students' complaints—"Why do I have to learn this?"—as they expressed their disinterest in Baroque and classical music. Our constant review of staff notation proved especially challenging for some of them. Much of my time was spent on behavior management, and when I got the pink slip at the end of the year stating that I had been laid off due to budget cuts, I was . . . relieved, sadly.

I optimistically assumed that I would be able to find a better music teaching position with a year's experience under my belt, but I had yet to land anywhere by the fall. Full-time jobs in the arts were hard to find at the time, so I took a job as a one-on-one support teacher for autistic students at a middle school. I was amazed by how much I learned about teaching students with disabilities and neurodiversity in just one year. It struck me: Why didn't I learn how to support students with special education needs in my teacher training? After all, music teachers often see all of the students in the school (or a large percentage of them) and often have very large classes. Large, inclusive classes!

For three years, I stayed in my support role. I observed that every one of my colleagues wanted the best for the students that I worked with. As an educator now working on the special education side of things, I started to notice that special education professionals frequently wondered why music teachers were not properly adapting for their students. Simultaneously, as a music educator, I heard from many music teachers that they were overwhelmed and not being supported enough in inclusion efforts. This seemed to be a common thread from school to school.

Unfortunately, most of my students got pulled from music class for academic support. This was the worst part: Students with social communication challenges or high anxiety were missing out on a class that benefited them and gave them a place where they could express themselves. I decided that I wanted to take steps to change this very common scenario.

That prompted me to go back to school to earn my master's in music education, with a focus on music for students with disabilities. I had learned a lot about adding supports, modifying materials, managing behavior, and communicating with students with disabilities in my one-on-one work. By the time I finished my master's degree, I was noticing common threads in research: Not only did methods and modalities need to be varied, but within each mode, there needed to be differentiation. Options were the key to student engagement and success.

After a brief stint as an elementary music teacher, I moved on to high school, where I thrived on teaching guitar, music technology, percussion, and popular music ensembles. I started to realize that my belief in popular music education was not only valid, it was far more relevant to my students than I had previously understood. Conversations in the field of music education on culturally responsive teaching, antiracist teaching, and accessible music education started to percolate. I started to find my stride as a music educator. I felt good about my ability to include students with low and high support needs in my classes, but I needed to learn more.

I enrolled in another graduate program solely focused on music education and students with autism. It was through that program that I discovered Universal Design for Learning (UDL). I became heavily focused on revamping the materials—especially the visuals—I used in the classroom. I researched the reasons why standard materials were inaccessible to students and started to create differentiated materials in response. I did a lot of work up front, but the classroom results were transformative. I no longer found myself spending a disproportionate amount of time helping one or two students make sense of their materials, while struggling to reach the rest of the class in the time that was left. Students were more independent and confident. The "Why do I need to know this?" queries became fewer and fewer.

As I found confidence in my teaching approach, my mission started to shift from "making music education accessible to students with disabilities" to "*helping teachers* to make music education accessible to students with disabilities." Eventually, as I became more rooted in my beliefs with regard to culturally responsive teaching, my goal shifted again to "helping teachers make music education accessible *to all students*."

I firmly believe we cannot help our students without helping our teachers—teachers like yourself. I hope you find this resource useful.

1

The Beginning Is the End

Universal Design for Learning (UDL) is a framework that, similar to the "backward design" model (Wiggins & McTighe, 2005), emphasizes the importance of starting with the learning goal. So, before you develop the recorder curriculum, ask yourself what the end goal is. This will make it possible to differentiate the engagement, representation, and assessment strategies through the lens of UDL.

As we all know, every teacher's reality is different. If your school is very focused on working with the national standards, keep in mind that national standards are written without knowledge of your unique teaching situation. For example, the National Core Arts Standards (NCAS) outline benchmarks for our students based on content area and grade level, detailing skills that qualify a high school student as achieving various levels of proficiency (novice, intermediate, proficient, etc.). These standards are available at www.nationalartsstandards.org.

I teach a lot of guitar classes, and many of my students have no experience with the instrument when they arrive in my class. Some have never played an instrument before in their lives! Not all of them even signed up for the class; they may have been placed there because of scheduling constraints. For various reasons, some will find playing chords very difficult and will need to approach them with simplified fingerings and strumming patterns. In addition, I do not see my students every day, and they do not take the instruments home with them because they are shared between all of my classes. These various factors mean that some of my students are unlikely to meet the NCAS benchmarks for proficiency in guitar at the high school level. However, I know my students. I know the context for which I am teaching. It is up to me to develop realistic and meaningful learning goals for my students and interpret how NCAS fits into those goals in a way that makes sense for them.

As you contemplate your learning goals, reflect on your own unique teaching situation. Determine what is reasonable and measurable for you and your students.

As we delve into each pillar of UDL (engagement, representation, and action and expression) in the following chapters, consider how UDL fits into your learning goals and activities. Many of the national standards will, and should, overlap with your goals. A UDL approach will deepen understanding for students, as it opens access points for a variety of learning styles and processes.

I encourage you to steep yourself in the UDL Guidelines, which are available at https://udlguidelines.cast.org and referenced throughout this book. The Guidelines are helpful for curriculum design and include dozens of prompts that will stimulate your thinking about how to make your units and lessons more inclusive and effective.

Questions to Ask Yourself as You Build Your Curricular Materials

- What do I want my students to know, and why? *(learning goal)*
- What types of activities can I offer my students to give them opportunities to develop the desired skills? *(learning activities)*
- Do my learning activities offer students different options for engaging with the material based on their individual strengths and interests, with choices regarding pacing, collaboration, and so on? *(engagement)*
- Do my learning activities present materials in a variety of formats? *(representation)*
- Do my learning activities allow students to express their knowledge through performance and written expression? Are students assessed using a variety of methods, with data collected via assessments used to make adjustments to pacing, learning goals, and methods? Are students offered modifications to the curriculum or learning goals, or added support to facilitate demonstration of their knowledge? *(action and expression)*

2

Engaging Students: Why Should I Take This Class?

As a new teacher, I learned quickly that I was on my own. I had about 35 students in my classes, many of whom had Individualized Education Programs (IEPs) or limited English proficiency, and I had no assistance. There was also no set curriculum. I could have seen the blank slate as an opportunity to teach whatever I wanted to. Instead, I taught what I thought I was "supposed" to teach: music theory and music history. In other words, how to read Western standard staff notation, and the history of Western European music from the Renaissance to the Romantic era. Though I tried to link the principles of sonata form and Gregorian chant to the popular music on the radio, I was flailing. Students' behaviors were off the wall. What was I missing?

Buy-in. All Grade 8 students had to take my class. What did they care about Bach? His music was of no relevance to them. The truth is, very real challenges aside, I failed to engage most of my students that year.

Why does engagement matter? If our students are engaged, they will likely have intrinsic motivation and interest in the material, commonly centered around a goal. This might be performance related, like a determination to learn a song by their favorite artist or take part in a concert. They might also want to be able to play songs casually, with friends or on their own, without performance pressure. The UDL Guidelines categorize the key components of engagement as recognizing and welcoming learners' unique interests and identities, sustaining effort and encouraging persistence, and developing skills and practices for self-regulation and self-assessment. That's how we get buy-in.

Looking back on my first year of teaching, I wish I could go back and tell my younger self to believe in the approach to music education that I had taken in private lessons, where the focus was often on the student's own musical interests. Our job is to spark engagement from our students. They don't owe us their attention; we need to earn it. Doing so requires attention to the environment we teach in, the students themselves, and the demands we place upon them.

Classroom Environment

The classroom environment has a lot to do with engagement or disengagement! Students with executive functioning challenges benefit from clear organizational patterns and consistency. Executive functioning impacts our ability to self-regulate, plan, transition, and remember (Hammel & Hourigan, 2013). Music classrooms can be a place of dysregulation for a lot of students due to differences in the classroom structure compared to other classes, more sensory stimuli, large class sizes, or other inevitable factors. If your class gets loud, allow students who are sensory defensive to wear headphones to dampen the noise. Many students who require special education support will have "preferential seating" listed on their IEPs. Traditional approaches have students seated by instrument, with the teacher at the front of the room. This can make it very difficult to accommodate preferential seating requirements. Getting creative with the physical placement of the students and the teacher in the classroom can not only boost student engagement but also boost your ability to assess how students are progressing. Move around the room, even if you are leading the students through a warmup or rehearsal piece! If your space allows for it, create a spot for students to rehearse and/or be assessed on their own—for example, by your desk, in the hall by the door, or in your office (if you have one).

Keeping a consistent class structure will benefit all students, but it's especially important for those with executive functioning challenges or limited language skills. Sometimes, students don't engage in a lesson because they don't know what to do or where to start. I start my classes with a warmup on the board, giving students 10 minutes to come into the classroom, get their instruments, and practice the warmup. Then, we rehearse the warmup together. Following that, we go into project-based learning or independent practice, and close with a wrap-up exercise and packing up. This consistent sequence of events supports students who may not know how to self-start or transition from one activity to the next.

Sometimes, I even give students a checklist for the day, outlining the agenda (Figure 2.1). Students who have trouble self-starting greatly benefit from this, as they are better able to engage with the material and less likely to feel overwhelmed when it is broken down in clear steps for them. For courses that utilize online resources, these checklists can also be digitized, with materials directly hyperlinked.

Classroom organization is also key to engagement. Students may not engage with a lesson because they can't find or don't have the materials they need. Students with organizational difficulties or working memory impairment may have a hard time remembering when your class meets or to bring the relevant materials on the appropriate

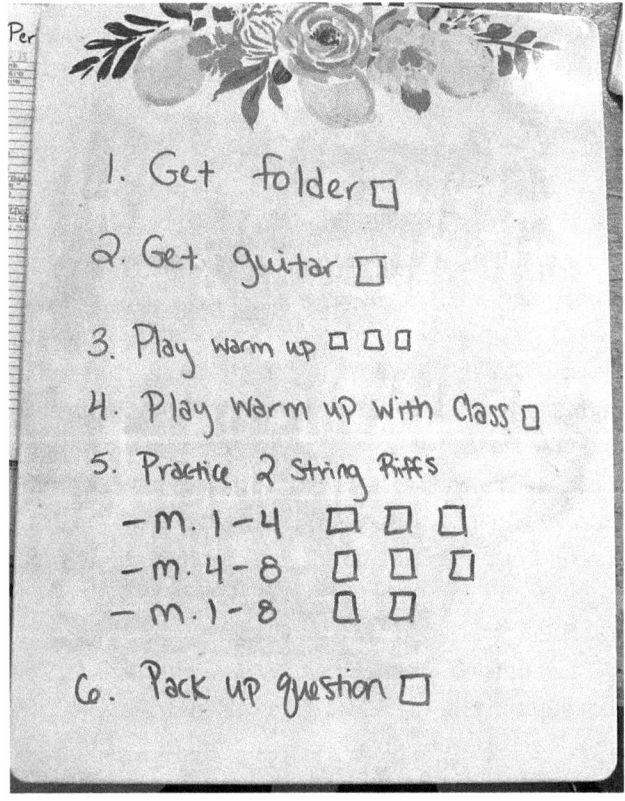

Figure 2.1. An example classroom agenda/checklist

day. I give all my students a place in the classroom to keep their music, and I make digital copies available online. Giving all students the option to store their materials in class destigmatizes the accommodation. In my classroom, all students are offered a folder for their music, and the folders are placed in a filing cabinet that is labeled and accessible to everyone. The instruments and the storage spaces for each instrument are numbered, and each student is assigned an instrument with a specific number. Materials such as pens, tuners, and guitar picks are stored in locations that are clearly labeled with both text and images (Figure 2.2). Providing labels in multiple forms and languages will benefit students with reading disabilities and English language learners.

Figure 2.2. Labeling materials clearly, using text and pictures, promotes accessibility.

Representation

Students can disengage with a class if they do not see themselves represented, or worse, find themselves marginalized. Take a look at your curricular materials. Are you including music that is performed and/or written by people of color? Women? Members of the LGBTQ+ community? The traditional music education curriculum tends to present a very homogeneous selection of composers and performers, and this can feel exclusionary to students who are not of the cisgender, white, non-disabled, male demographic.

In addition to music selection, consider how you assign students to particular instruments. Representation of certain instruments has historically been gendered, with some regarded as boys' instruments and others as girls'. This might lead a student to choose an instrument that doesn't interest them (or avoid one that does) out of pressure to conform to gender stereotypes. The same goes for certain ensembles and genres of music. For example, Wehr (2015) describes how female students in jazz bands experience high attrition rates due to the long-standing gender gap in this genre leading to feelings of tokenism, "stereotype threat" (a fear of confirming the belief that they shouldn't be included), and low self-efficacy (p. 475).

We have tremendous power as educators to dismantle these stereotypes when representation is presented without tokenism. Celebrate female musicians outside of women's history month, LGBTQ musicians outside of pride month, and so forth. Be mindful of what you show as examples of excellence when it comes to certain instruments or genres. Are all of the "rock and roll heroes" that you present to a class white men? Are the only women presented to the class singers? The internet is a gold mine of resources that can help you diversify examples of who can be a standard of excellence.

There are other ways that gender stereotypes can dampen engagement. For example, I used to address all my classes as "ladies and gentlemen." Then, a presentation from my school's Gay–Straight Alliance informed the staff that the automatic binary gendering of the student population was very alienating to some of its members. I now address my students differently: "Musicians! Guitarists! Lovely people of the music class!" There's no shortage of options that don't risk excluding anyone. Pay close attention to your games and activities, seating, and student selection processes as well. Are you grouping students by gender (boys in one group and girls in the other)? Are you asking students to take turns, "boy, girl, boy, girl"? These approaches assume a lot about our students without including their voices, creating an uncomfortable environment for some.

Being inclusive in language and practice greatly affects our students' ability to engage in class. In choir, for example, students are typically grouped by gender, but this may cause discomfort. As Miller (2016) points out, "The pitch of someone's voice can determine whether or not they 'pass' as their identified gender. Because transgender voices do not always match outward gender expression, trans people may be silenced from speaking or singing out of fear or embarrassment" (p. 61). Consider grouping students by voice, leaving gender out of the equation. Also, ensure that your dress codes for performances are not gender-specific.

Culturally Responsive Teaching

McKoy and Lind (2016) define culturally responsive teaching in music education as "the ability to affirm diverse cultural characteristics, perspectives, and experiences and to use these multiple perceptions of reality and ways of knowing to form bridges to new learning and ideas" (p. 17). This involves creating an environment where students' cultures are affirmed in the classroom, rather than them being expected to assimilate to the dominant culture. It also involves using multiple forms of communication, and understanding that cultural differences can affect how students interact with their education. For example, some students may come from cultures where learning by ear is the predominant way to learn music, whereas others may have experience with a fixed-do system. It's important that we understand and acknowledge perspective, rather than telling some students their approach is wrong; instead, we can build on their strengths and put their knowledge to use for developing new skills.

Providing students choices in music repertoire is imperative, whether it be working collaboratively on a concert program or allowing multiple options for practicing the same skill. For example, when I focus on teaching students the first two strings on the guitar, I pull guitar riffs from a variety of genres of music. The aim is to include at least one selection for each student that is familiar and, even better, interesting to them. I don't start from scratch every year, but rather alter my collection based on what new music the students are interested in and which riffs have fallen out of favor amongst the student body. Sometimes, I'm surprised by the difference between what I *think* will be popular practice options and what actually become popular practice options!

Pacing

Another element that can have a big impact on engagement is pacing. Providing options for practice material can also mean offering different levels of complexity, such as:

- Simplified parts for students in band or orchestra—for example, playing beat one of each measure instead of the full part. It is important that this option is offered to all, rather than it being seen as the "easy part" for a specific student. I have rarely found that students who don't need them will take simplified parts, and offering the choice to everyone destigmatizes them.

- Practice options in a piano class that all focus on the same scale or set of notes, but with varying difficulty of rhythm patterns.

- Practicing a chord progression in a guitar class with simplified chords, open chords, or bar chords.

You might want to provide students with space or time to practice at their own pace as well, rather than constantly making them keep up with the pace of the whole class. These moments, whether a small portion of a class or the bulk of the work time, can provide a valuable opportunity to "check in" with students. This strategy also accommodates students who are more advanced; for example, students who play string instruments can work on learning a piece in a new position to advance their fingerboard knowledge. Students can disengage in a class if it feels too easy or boring, just as they can if it seems too challenging.

Multiple Means of Engagement

As teachers, it is vital that we provide multiple means of engagement, taking into account our students' cultural backgrounds, their individual strengths and musical interests, and whether they require educational supports. What we present to our students, and how, holds a lot of power. We cannot expect students to participate if they feel marginalized, confused, misrepresented, or unsafe. This does take a lot of work on our end, and it hugely depends on who our students are, too! Pre-planning with regard to your classroom environment and curricular materials will be greatly helpful, but keep in mind that your plans may shift as the school year evolves and you get to know your students. Also keep in mind that all the examples presented in this book are just that: examples. There are lots of things that you can do to engage students who do, and do not, elect to be in your classroom.

Questions to Ask Yourself as You Develop Your Curricular Materials

Access: Do you provide options for welcoming interests and identities?

In a fifth-grade ukulele unit focused on practicing the C, F, and G chords, students are allowed to have independent practice time to pace themselves through a selection of songs. Offer songs from different genres and artists, being sure to include songs written or recorded by underrepresented identities.

Build: Do you provide options for sustaining effort and persistence?

In a bucket drumming unit for middle school general music, students are working on duets that include sixteenth and eighth note patterns. Offer duets that range in complexity, from consistent quarter note, quarter rest, eighth note pairs and sixteenth note groups that are mainly in unison to duets that include eighth and sixteenth note rests and other, more complex eighth and sixteenth note combinations. Allow students to choose their tempos. This will encourage engagement for students who need more processing time, or who may have difficulty with sixteenth note groupings. It will also allow for more advanced students to challenge themselves.

Internalize: Do you provide options for emotional capacity?

In a high school music class, the day's agenda is presented on the board, with small whiteboards and markers available for students who benefit from having checklists for the day's agenda, including checkboxes for each section to be rehearsed from each piece in the rehearsal. Write in breaks for students that might have trouble focusing or self-regulating, being sure to check in with those students between rehearsal benchmarks.

3

Represent!
What Is Music Literacy?

As a developing guitarist, I was very used to having a variety of forms of instruments, styles of playing, and formats of notation available to me. Guitarists played popular music and often learned by ear, chord charts, or a system called tablature. When I started my teaching career, however, I believed that every student needed to learn standard staff notation.

The ultimate goal of UDL is for all students to become expert learners who are knowledgeable and resourceful, strategic and goal-directed, and purposeful and motivated (Meyer et al., 2024). Reaching this goal requires presenting information in ways that are accessible to all students—in other words, providing multiple means of representation. The truth is, my insistence on staff notation was preventing some of my students from becoming expert learners, as was evident by their difficulty retaining and transferring their knowledge from class to class. These barriers were leading to frustration, disengagement, and behavior problems. I needed to expand my ideas of music literacy. I needed to think like a guitarist again!

This can be difficult work for music educators. It is time-consuming and challenges our traditions and training. However, I encourage you to think outside of the box. Through reevaluating my definition of music literacy, I was able to successfully implement an adapted music class for students with high support needs, including those with impaired processing speed or communication or fine motor skills.

When I started teaching adapted music, I wasn't quite sure what to do. I focused on syllables and created patterns using the students' favorite animals or foods. It was fun, but there wasn't any structure or scope and sequence to my curriculum. We used hand percussion instruments, but it was still a bit chaotic. Furthermore, I truly wasn't sure if any learning was happening. There was nothing measurable to assess my students on.

The next year, I decided to employ visuals. I used blocks to represent beats and a slide presentation to present one measure per slide. A stop sign indicated a rest. I included numbers underneath each box or rest (Figure 3.1). This allowed me to check for understanding with questions like "What beat is the rest on?" I eventually added eighth notes with half blocks, and I added words like "dog" and "puppy" to help the students hear the difference (Figure 3.2). I assessed with questions like "Which beat has a 'dog'?" and "Which beat has a 'puppy'?"

Figure 3.1. A measure, with blocks representing beats and a stop sign representing a rest

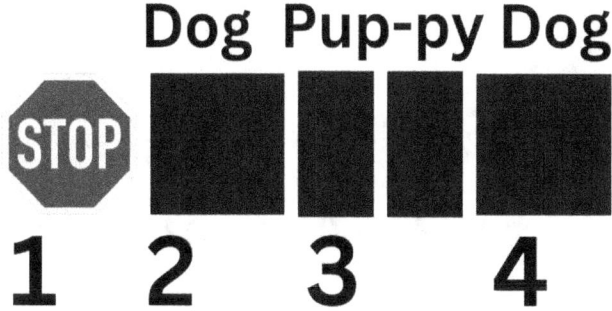

Figure 3.2. Adding eighth notes with half blocks and words to aid with comprehension

Our exploration of rhythms went from auxiliary percussion instruments, like shakers and claves, to drum pads. I added a black square to the middle of each drum pad with black-colored vinyl, and added an X to the rim of the drum pad (Figure 3.3). I then started teaching my students simple snare drum patterns using the same symbols (Figure 3.4). They did well! They were now not just understanding that the shape of an image could denote duration, but that the way it looked could denote *where* on the instrument they would play.

Figure 3.3. A drum pad marked up with two shapes

Figure 3.4. Using those shapes to denote where on the instrument to play

We eventually got to the point where I could not fill a whole class with rhythm practice anymore. I decided to take my students to the musical instrument digital interface (MIDI) keyboards that I used for my music technology courses. I added three different strips of colored vinyl on the middle C, D, and E keys (later adding more colors to fill the octave, as in Figure 3.5). I purposefully didn't use the Boomwhackers colors because I only wanted one variant of each color, to account for inconsistencies in computer screen and printing hues. Again showing one measure per slide, I created a slide deck of "Hot Cross Buns" using the same block notation that I had used for rhythm—but this time, I filled the blocks in with colors (Figure 3.6).

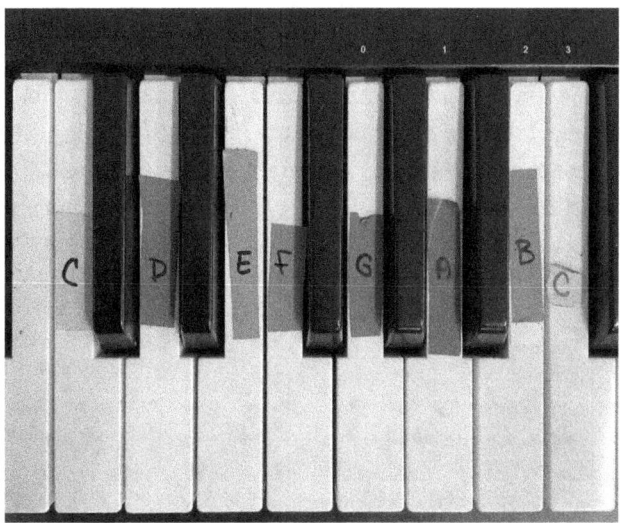

Figure 3.5. A MIDI keyboard marked up with strips of colored vinyl

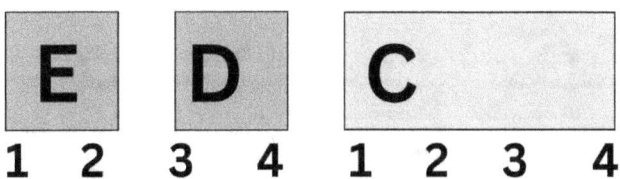

Figure 3.6. A slide from the "Hot Cross Buns" slide deck, using colored block notation

I found that, with a little bit of demonstration and support, the students were able to navigate through the slides. They became increasingly independent the more we practiced using the slides, often moving through the slide deck themselves. I started adding blocks that were twice as long to represent half notes, and blocks that were four times as long to represent whole notes. I found that most of the students were able to purposefully press down and hold the keyboard keys when they interpreted the two- and four-beat blocks.

After I'd been teaching the adapted music class for two years, my students moved on from three-pitch melodies to five-pitch melodies, full octave melodies, melodies that go beyond one octave and use sharps and flats (using different shapes to denote a different octave), and finally to practicing full chords (Figure 3.7). Some students moved

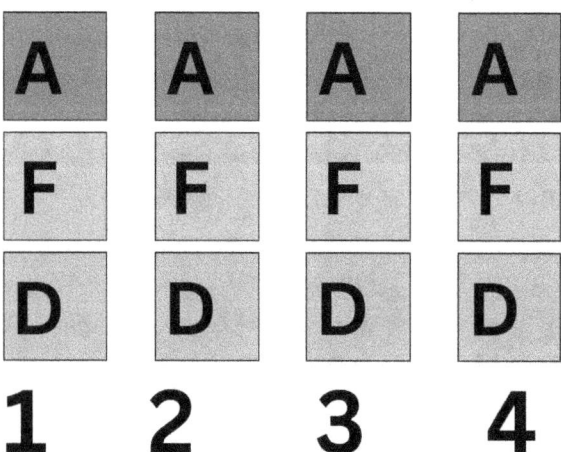

Figure 3.7. A full chord in colored block notation

on to reading color-coded staff notation, connecting the direction of the notes in the notation to the direction of the keys on the MIDI keyboard. Their advancement was truly amazing, and I strongly believe that it was largely due to the flexibility I gave them in the visuals that I presented.

The Reasons for Options in Music Literacy Visuals

Shifting away from requiring all students to read staff notation takes a willingness to step away from traditional approaches and adopt a broader view of what is considered music literacy. Let me be clear that I am not advocating for removing staff notation from the classroom. Rather, I am advocating for dismantling an approach that considers staff notation to be the *only* acceptable form of music literacy. It might be helpful to understand why.

First, standard staff notation is not very instinctual. For instance, one study found that the majority of nonmusicians believe that a whole note represents a rest, rather than an eighth rest, because it is "empty" (Tan et al., 2009, p. 14). In fact, an overwhelming number of participants "tended to associate height of symbol on the vertical axis with pitch, proximity of notes along the horizontal axis with speed, and size of symbol with loudness" (p. 18). However, that is not how standard staff notation functions at all.

Second, reading standard staff notation requires a significant amount of decoding and working memory, skills that will be challenging for students who struggle with executive functioning (Hammel & Hourigan, 2013). Students on the autism spectrum, with ADD/ADHD, or with specific learning disabilities such as dyslexia have executive dysfunction. (Their IEPs will tell you.)

Understanding staff notation requires more than decoding and memorization, however. Take for consideration the steps required to read, understand, and apply staff notation:

1. Differentiate the (usually) black notes from the (usually) black lines to decipher what symbol we are looking at.
2. Decode the shape of the symbol (note) and remember what that means for its duration.
3. Determine whether the symbol is on a line or space.
4. Recall what letter that line or space is assigned, depending on the clef.
5. Recall what that letter infers with regard to fingering and/or embouchure on the instrument being played.

These steps require us to be able to differentiate foreground from background, read images of a certain size, decode symbols, recall memorized information, read information on uneven plains, and more. That's a lot to process.

Visual information that is straightforward will be most helpful. There are many ways to approach this. When adapting notation, consider changes in color, shape, direction, and size. As a musician, you are a creative person, so developing adapted notations may come easily to you. However, I'd like to propose some ideas that I have found useful for my classroom:

- Enlarge the visuals and eliminate any information that the student is not using.

- Add color to help differentiate notes from lines.
- Add color to reinforce finger placement on the instrument (color-code).
- Use shapes that infer duration rather than standard rhythmic notation.
- Combine shapes and colors to denote pitch and rhythm, and possibly remove the horizontal movement of the notes altogether.

Auditory Versus Visual Learning

There are many methods of teaching music that rely significantly on auditory learning, such as Suzuki and Conversational Solfege. Some students will excel in an auditory mode of learning. Many of my students come from cultural backgrounds where music is learned by listening and showing, so this feels natural to them. Some, however, struggle. I came to learn this the hard way when I had a student with dyslexia in guitar class. I assumed that reading the music was hard for them, so I removed the barriers of reading staff notation and gave them color-coded tablature to go along with their color-coded guitar. I determined that they would learn the rhythms of the practice piece by listening to me play it in a call and response fashion. The student struggled to imitate me.

After a bit of research, I found that some people with specific learning disabilities have difficulty perceiving rhythmic duration (Overy et al., 2003). This can also be true of anyone with executive dysfunction (Lesiuk, 2015). Students with processing delays may struggle with auditory information too, if it is too fast and they have no reference to look back on after the auditory information is gone. It is important to remember that every student is different and cannot be defined solely by their cultural background or diagnosis.

I determined that my guitar student with dyslexia needed a visual to help them track the duration of each note. Western notation required too much decoding, but relying solely on auditory learning was not equitable because it wasn't giving them enough support. I developed a form of tablature that used a colored block system, much like I used on piano, to represent fret and duration. This way, the student still benefited from using a tablature system and colors to support their finger placement, with the added benefit of a very concrete representation of length of note (Figure 3.8).

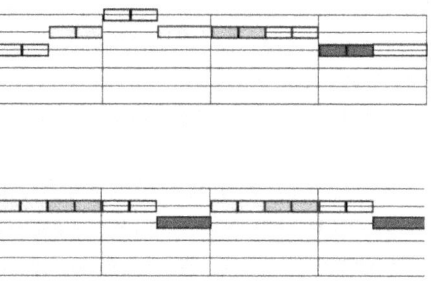

Figure 3.8. The colored block system for guitar

Multiple Means of Representation

Providing multiple means of representation is important to accommodate the strengths and needs of all students, as there is no single means that will be optimal for everyone. Every sighted student needs to have a meaningful visual form of representation available to them, as well as an auditory and kinesthetic representation. Not every student will use each mode, and that's okay. This goes for all of the information we give our students, not just information on learning a piece of music. I verbally tell my students what my instructions are, as well as writing them down and actively demonstrating them. If you have access to technology, creating step-by-step guides in slide format can be really helpful for students who find success with small chunks of information. This allows me to write instructions in multiple languages and breaks down assignment steps in a format that students can always refer back to. Both are helpful for English learners and students with disabilities. Most programs will have a text-to-speech function, if you are unable to read the instructions to students who benefit from auditory instruction. I have found this approach helpful when assigning projects to students.

Questions to Ask Yourself as You Develop Your Curricular Materials

Access: Do you provide options for perception?

In a beginning piano class, offer students a recording that they can refer to when learning their assignments. Provide practice sheets in double-sided handouts with letter names in the noteheads on one side, and the other side without. Add colored vinyl strips on each piano keyboard to correspond with each pitch, and give students highlighters to color-code their music if need be.

Build: Do you provide options for language and symbols?

In a third-grade general music class, students are learning B-A-G on the recorder. They're reading staff notation with letter noteheads to start. Some students may use color coding to correspond with colored reinforcer stickers around each finger hole. Other students who struggle with decoding rhythmic notation are able to use block notation, where one block denotes one beat, a block twice as long denotes two beats, and so on. A stop sign indicates a rest. Students are also offered one-on-one demonstrations or pictures of hands on the recorder to represent each note, with written instructions available in multiple languages.

Internalize: Do you provide options for building knowledge?

Give students a vision board every term that illustrates what they have learned and what they are going to learn. Let them trace their skills with the text and images at the start of every unit so that they can track their progress and see the connections.

4

How Do We Know They Know?

In my development as a musician, my progress was often assessed through a performance: A demonstration during a lesson. A studio recital. A jazz band concert. A semester jury. A big band concert. A senior recital. Chances are, much of this sounds familiar to you, too. Many of us have moved through a process, as both a musician and a music educator, where assessment equals performance. It's generally acknowledged that this makes sense: If you can play through the music, then you understand the concepts. However, while music is very performance-oriented, it does not necessarily have to be.

In my second year of teaching high school, I came across a student with selective mutism. Again, keep in mind that not all of my students sign up to be in my class. Or perhaps this student had an interest in playing music, but not for others. I was stumped as to how to assess the student when it came time for the typical assignments I had embedded in my curriculum. I could tell that they were doing well during independent practice, but whenever I came to their side, they would stop playing. If I asked a clarifying question, they would act as if they didn't know what I was talking about. I believed they did know, but just couldn't demonstrate it in the way I was suggesting: a fretboard quiz for which they had to play the note or chord I was requesting, the performance assignment that they had to play (just for me), or the composition project that they not only had to write but also had to play through (just for me).

I developed a process for this student: For fretboard or chord quizzes, they had the option to fill out a fretboard diagram. For a performance-based assessment, they could do a recording for me via their phone or the (at the time) class iPad. If it was a duet performance, they would record themselves playing along with a recording of me playing the opposite part. Through these differentiated approaches, the student was able to demonstrate that they understood the material. An added benefit was that they became more comfortable with me, because they saw that I was willing to accommodate their needs. Eventually, they would occasionally talk to me.

Performance-based assessments can be daunting for some students, for various reasons. They may have anxiety. They may have slow processing speed. Or they may just not be all that interested. Do all of your students want to be performers? Did they choose to take the class, or was it required? I have had students placed in my performance-based ensembles who had no intention of getting on stage and performing for other people. The challenge then is to find a way to assess their work while also meeting them where they are in terms of access points and goals.

What Is a Musician? A Composer?

Providing options for expression means that teachers need to include room for flexibility in their assessment methods, so that they can be consistent and predictable in evaluating their students. We may need to ask ourselves how we define an "instrument," a "musician," and a "composer." Is our definition of an instrument dependent on a specific genre of music, or what the instrument is made of, or how much it costs? Is our definition of a composer dependent on a specific form of music literacy or genre? Does our definition of a musician hinge on an individual having certain physical traits or abilities? Once I started to consider these kinds of questions, I quickly realized that there were some ugly truths behind my preconceived notions.

Instrumentation is one key element that is quickly becoming more accessible, if we allow ourselves to expand our definition of "real" instruments beyond "physical" instruments. Virtual instruments, both web-based and app-based, are constantly growing in capabilities as well as variety. If a student has difficulty with fine motor skills, a virtual instrument can offer accessibility and choice in ways that a physical instrument cannot. For example, a student with impaired left hand mobility might find that a virtual guitar allows them better access to a guitar class curriculum. Many virtual guitars also offer options for playing chords, as well as a variety of guitar sounds (nylon, acoustic, or electric); some even offer the possibility of recording work as a WAV or MP3 file, which is great for assessment purposes. Teachers can also simplify the presentation of some virtual instruments, either through the options of the program itself or through settings like "guided access" on an iPad. A low-tech approach could involve developing paper screens with cutouts that simplify the view on a device for the student.

The example in Figure 4.1 demonstrates how a virtual instrument on an iPad can utilize color coding to correspond with visuals. A student using a virtual guitar still needs to understand how to read the notation, learn how to play in time, and develop technique on their instrument, much like a student using a physical guitar.

Technology also offers a variety of ways in which students can demonstrate an understanding of dynamics, duration, and pitch. There are many websites and apps that offer music creation capabilities, from drum machines and beat making applications to programs and sites for Western standard staff notation composition. Students working in a digital audio workstation (DAW) that allows the ability to record with MIDI instruments, add loops or samples, and arrange patterns within drum machines are able to demonstrate understanding of various composition aspects without working in Western

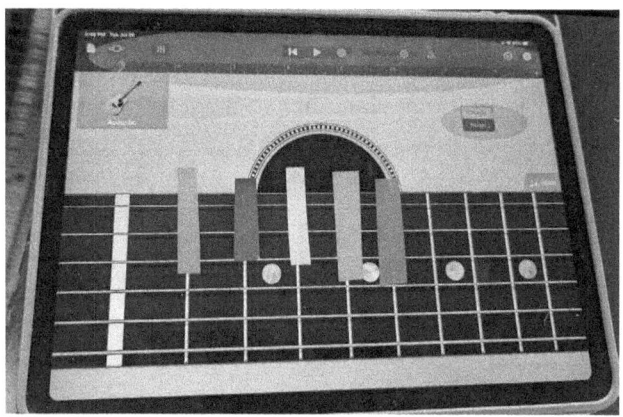

Figure 4.1. Color coding on a virtual guitar using colored vinyl on the iPad

notation. See Figure 4.2 for an example of MIDI piano roll in GarageBand. Can you tell how many measures are presented? How long each note lasts? The pitch? Visual representations of musical elements in digital music platforms might be more meaningful to some students than traditional representations. This especially depends on the genre of music and instrumentation they prefer. Consider this when determining what "composition" or "music literacy" means in your classroom.

While technology is increasingly helpful for including students of all abilities in classroom activities, we must also consider what is accessible to *us*, the teachers, when considering our tools. Not every teacher will have access to high-tech, or even mid-tech, tools. Low-tech materials can allow alternative forms of composition for assessment purposes too. For example, students in my adapted music course composed via colored sticky notes on paper templates (Figure 4.3). This approach offered a low-tech tool for composition, with options for size and complexity, that directly correlated with pitch (color) and rhythm (length of block). Using tactile materials worked best for my students because computer tools were too difficult to navigate at the time. I also did the same with icon

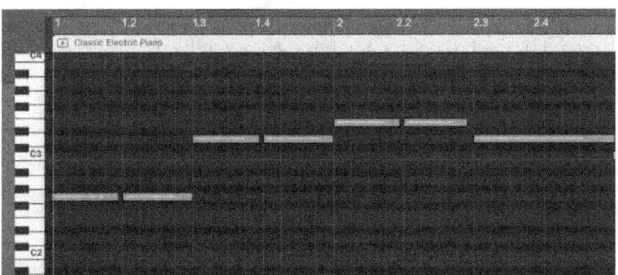

Figure 4.2. MIDI piano roll in GarageBand

notation for percussion using Velcro, beat grids, and small rhythmic pattern cards that students could move to their chosen beat and measure.

In addition to making music learning more accessible to people with disabilities, technology can enhance accessibility through cultural relevance. Many of our students are engaging with music that is created digitally. It is therefore our responsibility to give them tools to express their musicality in a way that connects with the music

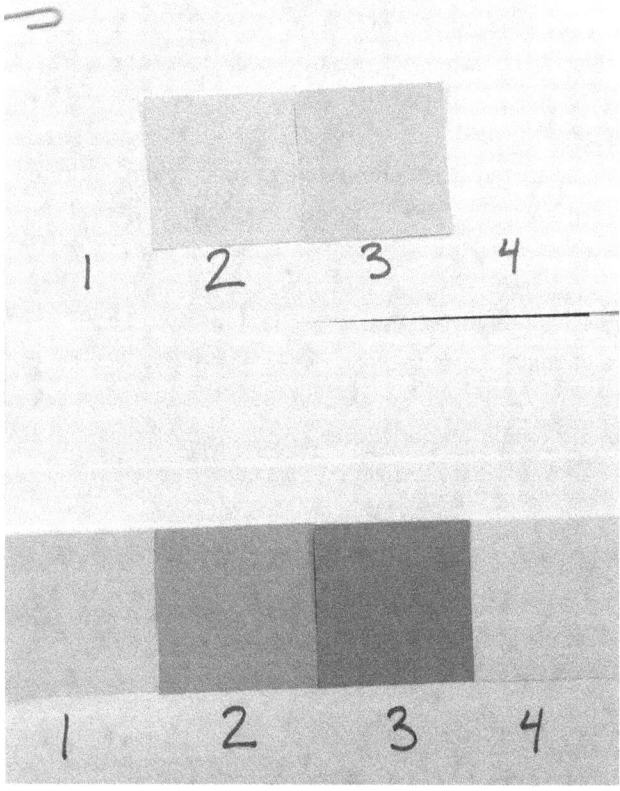

Figure 4.3. A low-tech tool for composition using colored sticky notes

that they are interested in. Composing in treble clef might be a meaningful experience for a student learning to play the flute in band class, but what about the student who is creating beats and collaborating with others online? Remembering the earlier discussion of starting with the learning goal: What do we want our students to know? If a learning goal is composing music in duple meter using a blues scale, students can demonstrate that skill in a multitude of ways.

Options for Action and Expression

Options for action and expression in music education extend beyond what tools we offer our students for playing and composing music. As the UDL Guidelines indicate, we should provide students with varied options for setting goals and planning, organizing, and monitoring their work (executive functions), as well as different options (media, methods, and tools) for expressing what they know, including assistive technologies if needed.

Consider the process of learning a piece of music. Have you ever encountered

- a student who always practices a piece from start to finish, making the same mistakes every time;
- a student who says, "But I already practiced that last time" when encouraged to practice a familiar piece; or
- a student who does not initiate practice on their own?

These students may not understand what skills we want them to develop, what progress they are making, or where to begin. In addition to supporting engagement for students, checklists, templates, and prompts also offer ways for us to break down information and processes for our students. Again, remember the learning goals that you are aiming for. If the goal is "all students will be able to play a five-note melody on their string instrument" and you have given them options for what they can play, that's great. But how do they get to their end goal? Furthermore, how do they know they are making good progress toward reaching their goal? Reflections and self-assessments, progress journals, and checklists can help a student develop skills in self-monitoring and help them achieve the learning goal.

Helping students self-monitor and work toward their goals also requires teachers to be up-front about how we are assessing them. Assessing in the arts can be tricky. Skills can be broken down into seemingly non-artistic categories, often leading us to ask ourselves whether we value the mechanics of making music over the artistic expression of the art. How do we assess artistic expression? However you decide to do so, be sure that your feedback is consistent and clear to the students in that it clearly spells out the criteria for success and the options they have for demonstrating their success.

UDL emphasizes the need to ensure that students have many ways to accomplish their learning goals. If you are allowing your students options in how they physically approach their instruments due to accessibility needs, ensure that grading rubrics align with those options. For example, it is not uncommon for performance-based assessments to require specific physical or cognitive skills of the musician, taking into account fingerings, posture, how a musician holds an instrument, or whether the music is memorized. Consider creating a rubric that all students, regardless of accommodations, can score well on, rather than having to modify rubrics on a case-by-case basis. Modifications will undoubtedly be required from time to time, but embedding accessibility in your rubrics will create more equity across the board. For example:

- Rather than focusing on fingerings in a guitar chord assessment, focus on whether the student is fretting the correct pitches. This will allow students to use simplified, open, or bar chord finger work. Students can still receive guidance on advancing finger work where appropriate, but are not marked down if they do not have the physical ability to use multiple fingers at once.

- Rather than focusing on standing posture for a choir, consider assessing elements of posture that can be demonstrated while standing or sitting (for example, shoulders and neck placement). This will allow for the inclusion of students who cannot stand.

- When appropriate, allow for student choice in tempo on their performance-based assessments. This will improve accessibility for students with processing delays. Instead, focus on steady beat and accurate pitches and rhythms.

Think about your learning goal and what makes sense for your teaching scenario. You can work with students on a case-by-case basis on fingerings, but if you are working with a class of students that are preparing for college auditions, then fingerings might be important. As teachers, we need to balance our duty to support all of our students with our responsibility to prepare our students for the expectations of future institutions.

Multiple Means of Action and Expression

Providing multiple options for action and expression should include how we allow our students to express themselves both musically and non-musically. Students should be able to express their needs via vocal communication, written communication, symbols, and any communication devices that are made available within the school. When embedding self-reflection into class practice, students should be able to communicate their thoughts through physical actions, verbal responses, or visuals. The same approaches can apply when expressing musical ideas; for example, when assessing students on identifying sol-mi patterns in a general music class, students might use Curwen hand signs, or point to pictures of the hand signals or solfege syllables, to demonstrate that they can identify the pitch. By providing a variety of ways for students to express their knowledge, we also provide ourselves with a variety of ways to assess a student's progress. This can be especially valuable when we have large classes and can spend a limited amount of time with each student.

Always keep your goals in mind. Is it most important to you that your students can play a G chord with three or four fingers, or that they can play a G chord? Is the end goal that students learn staff notation, or that they learn to play a melody on piano in the key of F major with expressive dynamics? In a choral class, is the emphasis on memorizing music, or on the cultural and expressive elements of the music? Once you determine what is important, you can develop a myriad of ways for your students to demonstrate their progress. Tracking students' progress in this way also informs educators on how effective our methods are and whether we need to adjust to create more access points.

Questions to Ask Yourself as You Develop Your Curricular Materials

Access: Do you provide options for interaction?

In a piano lab class, students can explore beginning melodies with one finger, all five fingers, and combinations in between. Practice pieces of varying degrees of complexity are included so that students who are just beginning to navigate the keyboard have an access point, but students who are more advanced are not bored. Work with each student on their individual progress in fingerings, being sure that healthy approaches are taken. Assess student work with regard to pitch, tempo, and rhythmic and dynamic accuracy.

Build: Do you provide options for expression and communication?

In a music history class, students are having a group debate on intellectual property lawsuits regarding hip-hop and pop music samples. Students can contribute to the class discussion by vocally speaking up, responding to prompts through gestures (thumbs up or thumbs down), adding ideas to sticky notes or whiteboards, or adding ideas to a shared online document. Students have the option of using translation services or text-to-speech devices as well.

Internalize: Do you provide options for strategy development?

In a ukulele class, students record progress in daily practice journals. They are able to make audio and video recordings, or simply write notes on what they accomplished in class. Students also have the option of tracking their progress at home if they have access to an instrument and practice after school hours. At the start of each practice session in class, students reflect first on the progress they made the last time they practiced, in relation to the final assessment goals.

5

Just a Note Before You Go

A common comment that I get when reviewing UDL with both pre-service and practicing teachers is, "This is a lot of work." This is often followed up by questions like "Won't this lead to more teacher burnout? I'm stretched thin already!" and "But won't the materials get too busy if you are implementing all of these options?" My answer to all of these comments and questions is a resounding "Yes!" Allow me to elaborate.

This *Is* a Lot of Work

It truly is, but it doesn't have to happen overnight. UDL is a framework; it's an approach to teaching that you can carry with you from year to year and continue to grow. There's a chance that you are already implementing a lot of these ideas. I was first introduced to UDL in my second round of graduate school—I had already completed an undergraduate degree, taught for seven years, and gone through my first graduate program. As I worked through a UDL template that was assigned to me, applying it to my guitar class elective, I started to notice that I wasn't coming up with much new material. There was a lot I was already doing; I just hadn't attached the name "Universal Design for Learning" to it. Ask yourself:

- Do I tend to offer a variety of music in the classroom for various activities?
- Do I tend to offer different levels of complexity in practice materials or parts, toward the same curricular goal?
- Do I check in with students with IEPs or Section 504 plans, and offer extra support for pacing and executive functioning?
- Do I tend to color-code, add fingerings, or offer visuals other than standard notation for music literacy opportunities?
- Do I tend to teach with a multimodal approach?
- Have I used technology for assessment purposes, to allow for adjustments in pacing and extra time?

If you answered yes to even one of these questions, then you're already on the road to teaching with UDL. If you didn't, no worries. Ask yourself if you *want* to say yes to any of these questions.

My arsenal of ideas and materials did not develop overnight, and they are not fixed or finished. I'll stick with guitar class for the sake of example. My first step in deciding that I wanted to overhaul my curriculum through the framework of UDL was to think about what I was already doing. I discovered that:

Engagement   I was already offering different genres and levels of complexity for my students, mainly with their practice materials.

Representation   I was offering staff and tab notation, with room for color coding and other adapted notations, but was requiring all students to read staff notation.

Action and expression   I was offering students the option to present via video, with extra time, or using other accommodations, on a one-on-one basis.

The next step was to fill in the gaps. By looking at what I was already doing, I was able to see what I was missing. A lot of the work in differentiating assessment and representation was happening on an individual basis, which often meant that it was taking away from my teaching time. For example:

A student is reading staff notation but, due to processing time and working memory deficits, requires significant support in reading the sheet. As I work around the room to help students during their independent practice time, I find myself stopped in my route as I work with this student. I review how to read the staff, work with them to label the notes, and then continue the process to decode where those notes are on their guitar. They write in the fingerings above the music. We work on some color coding. I give them an extension of practice time, as I have a date set for the "performance" assessment of the assignment. By the time I am done working with this student, I have just 10 minutes left to help any others.

If this scenario sounds familiar to you, you might sympathize with the stress of the situation. Raised hands that I wasn't getting to, students disengaging because I wasn't checked in with them . . . there was a lot of work I wasn't able to do in that moment because my curriculum was not very accessible to *one* student. Designing the curriculum with the UDL principles in mind would have taken a bit more preparation up front, but it would have resulted in less work once the students were in my classroom, thus allowing me to check in with more students more effectively. What I needed to do to shift from a multimodal, differentiating teaching approach to a truly *UDL* teaching approach was:

Engagement Embed variety within my assigned pieces in relation to genre, composer representation, and complexity. I was offering variety with my guitar riff and chord practice, but when it came time for performance assignments, students were being assessed on pieces from a very homogeneous background. This not only impacted engagement but also spoke volumes about what my curriculum valued, which was not the message I wanted to send.

Representation Allow students to choose the mode of literacy that makes sense for them as it relates to disability, cultural relevance, and musical goals. This includes offering materials in multiple formats for all students, and offering guidance for students who aren't sure what their preference is.

Action and expression Allow students a variety of options for performance and project assignments (e.g., in person or via video) that they can finish within a timeline, rather than one date for completion. This allows for self-pacing, as well as room for retries and self-reflection for students that want to continue refining their work.

Front-loading this work is essential, but it doesn't have to be done all at once. Shifting my approach to assessment was largely a structural change. The bulk of the work was adjusting my teaching materials and the formats I presented them in. I started by subbing out one current performance option for a new piece from a different genre each quarter. I shifted my expectations regarding staff notation, and instead offered students handouts with both staff and tab notation, checking in often in warmup and wrap-up exercises to ensure that they could tell the difference, regardless of their preference. The next year, I replaced one more piece each quarter. Over the course of the year, each time I got to a new unit, I worked on creating a digital collection of every practice piece in color and black and white. I share the documents with students and give them markers so that they can color-code their handouts if they find that helpful. I color-code the frets on half of the guitars in the classroom so that they are readily available to students who prefer to use them. Every year, I find that I spend less time on planning and more on finding new and exciting teaching materials. During class time, I find I am spending less time trying to get kids started, reviewing the same material (like music literacy), or trying to get them to the finish line. Overall, students are spending more time practicing and developing their technique.

I'm Already Stretched Thin

This is the reality for many teachers. If implementing a UDL mindset in your class feels overwhelming, start by focusing on one area rather than overhauling your whole approach at once. Doing a little bit is better than doing nothing at all, and with practice, UDL will begin to feel more accessible. Also, remember that following the UDL

Guidelines means giving students options, but it doesn't have to mean that you offer every option under the sun. The aim of providing options is developing expert learners, not accommodating every student's smallest desire (keep in mind that this is different from providing the accommodations or modifications specified in an IEP, which we are legally obligated to do). Here's an example of where I had to draw the line for myself:

In a guitar class, I was starting students on one-string guitar riffs using tab notation. They had a few different songs to choose from, and the goal was to engage them in playing something they could recognize, while allowing room for pacing and the development of skills needed to navigate moving up and down the fretboard. One particular student was already using a smaller, nylon string guitar with color coding. However, they had read staff notation in middle school in their general music class, and they really liked the consistency of it because of the rhythm symbols. I offered to write the rhythm symbols over the tab notation, or to let the student use the color block tab notation that I had available through an online document.

I could tell that this student was able to read the tab notation and apply it; they were able to play the guitar riffs well. However, they soon became stuck on the rhythmic aspect of reading tablature, and started requesting more and more accommodations on their handouts. I was spending a lot of prep time creating a special grid system for this one student, when it occurred to me: Realistically, they wouldn't have so many accommodations if they wanted to find a guitar tab online. They could read the tab just fine; they just didn't like that it was a bit abstract with respect to rhythmic interpretation. I asked them: Is this a "want" or a "need"? The conclusion was that it was a "want." So, I moved the student back to tablature for guitar riffs, because they had acquired the necessary skills. They continued reading both staff and tab that year and would often write in rhythmic notation on their paper with a pencil for their own reference.

This is an example of a scenario where I could have run myself ragged differentiating material for a student, but where I wasn't actually helping them develop self-regulation and persistence. As teachers, our desire to help can lead to scenarios like this. Check in with yourself often on the "why" of the options you are providing.

Won't the Materials Get Too Busy If You Are Implementing All of These Options?

This is a valid point! I like to double-side single handouts with visual options, use technology when possible, and offer different versions of the same handout when possible. However, when presenting materials to the class as a whole, this becomes more difficult. Take, for example, a warmup that I am projecting on the board, like a major scale in a beginner piano skills class. I might use a few options here, such as:

- Color-coding the notes on the staff, with note names labeled and counting underneath. Students can use the colors if they find them helpful, but I have never found that the students who don't need them getting distracted. The same goes for the note names. As I lead students through the warmup, I might call out the counting as I play along, or the note names and colors. It's important to run through the warmup a few times at a few different tempos.

- Offering printed versions of the warmups for students that prefer having materials on their music stands. Students can color-code or label these as needed. I then present the warmup on the board with minimal support, but still call out the counting, note names, or colors as I'm guiding the students through it. This minimizes the visual stimuli on the board (the "too cluttered" factor) while providing verbal tracking for students who benefit from supports.

- Using laminated staff paper that allows me to prepare color-coded or labeled versions of the warmup ahead of class. At the start of class, I check in with my students and offer the laminated warmups as an option. I have never been in a situation where the whole class requests this accommodation, even though I offer it to everyone! Usually, it's just a handful of students. Again, I then present the warmup on the board with minimal support, calling out the counting, note names, or colors to guide them as we run through it.

One More Thing

Remember why you became a musician. There is magic in music! It sounds cheesy, but isn't it true? Then, remember why you decided to *teach* music. You were likely motivated by principles such as self-expression, advocacy, social justice, inclusion, creativity, and critical thinking. Music is a part of all of our identities. Our musical preferences evolve with us as we grow and age. They say a lot about who we are and what we believe, and working with students as they develop their musical identities is powerful work. UDL is just one way in which we can ensure that every student, regardless of cultural background, economic background, gender identity, disability, or overall learning style, has access to developing their own musical identity.

My experiences are unique to my teaching environment, and I hope I have made that clear. Your experience will be different, depending on the ages of your students, where you teach, and the content area you work with. Your path in UDL will not look the same as mine, just as mine looks different from those that I learned from. And it will never be perfect. Teaching never is. We are constantly reflecting, adjusting, and improving. Although there are some definite wrong approaches, in teaching there is no one right approach that works for every student. I've been told by supervisors that part of what makes our job so difficult is that it is a "human profession." That sounds odd, but I understand what they mean. We aren't working with codes and machines. We aren't working with math equations, where there is always one right answer to the problem. We are working in fluid situations, with human beings that are developing. Our work is often unpredictable and constantly changing. We adapt a lot, and our approach should, too.

I am, by no means, the paragon of UDL teaching. I am always working to be a better teacher. To be honest, it's exhausting, but I probably don't need to tell you that! The fact that you picked up this book and have taken this time to reflect on your practice means that you are doing the work to become a better teacher, too. I hope this book has given you some ideas on how you can tweak your pedagogy and curriculum to make them even more accessible than they already are. We are creative individuals, after all—we are artists! Getting creative in how we teach music is just another strength we can develop.

6

Sample Lessons

Sample Lesson: Guitar

Grade level/ensemble: Middle school or high school general music/guitar

Objectives: Students will be able to demonstrate lead guitar skills using two (high E and B) strings of the guitar in a level of rhythmic and pitch diversity that fits their experience level.

Number of classes for lesson: Two to four

Background information needed for this lesson: Students should already have experience using one and two strings of the guitar to practice rhythmic and melodic patterns. Students should also have experience reading tablature and staff notation. Regardless of which they find most accessible and/or relevant, it is important that students are able to differentiate between the two. I suggest building student skills and engagement before this lesson through the use of one- and two-string guitar riffs of varying levels of rhythmic, pitch, and fret position diversity.

Give students two to four classes to practice guitar riffs from rock, pop, classical, and hip-hop songs, ensuring they each have something of personal music interest to work with and use to develop their lead skills.

NCAS: The following anchor standards are addressed:

- Anchor Standard 4: Select, analyze, and interpret artistic work for presentation.
- Anchor Standard 6: Convey meaning through the presentation of artistic work.
- Anchor Standard 7: Perceive and analyze artistic work.

Procedure:

1. Begin class with a warmup review of notes B, C, D, E, F, and G on the first and second strings on the board. Present the warmup in color-coded staff and tab notation. Students will get their guitars and start the warmup as soon as they enter the classroom. Use this time to assess who might need extra help, or a copy of the warmup on their music stand.

2. Once all students have had a chance to review the warmup independently or with you, get the class's attention. First, ask the students to name three differences between staff and tab notation (acceptable answers: staff has rhythm symbols and tab has numbers, staff has five lines and tab has six lines, staff has a treble clef, staff has notes on lines and spaces while tab has notes on the lines only). Then, review the note names and locations as a class. Students might demonstrate their knowledge by responding verbally or physically showing where each note is when called upon.

3. Next, review the duration of each note. Depending on which day of the lesson you are on, you might tackle a quarter note, half note, or whole note exercise. Emphasize that tab notation does not give much information in regard to note duration. Note the space between the notes and how many beats there are per measure (four).

4. Ask students for the first note of the warmup exercise. Students might respond verbally or by demonstrating on their guitars. Inform students that the class will now play the warmup together, on the count of four. Count the class in and play through the exercise. Call out the beats or the note names, depending on which support the students seem to benefit from most. This will allow for verbal tracking that matches the visual, for students that benefit from tracking. As the class plays the exercise, use this time to assess who is and isn't following along.

5. After running through the exercise once, ask students how the pacing felt. They can reply verbally or with a nonverbal gesture, like a thumbs up, down, or sideways.

6. Play the exercise once more, taking into consideration the feedback from the students. Again, assess the class to identify students who may not be following along this time around. Some students may have needed more time to process, and you may find they are following along now.

7. Inform the students that they will now go into their independent practice of "La Bamba" or "Ode to Joy." Demonstrate the options on the guitar if you have

not yet, giving background as to how both selections have become protest songs of social movements. Ask the students if they know of any other protest songs, and what movements they represent. Allow students to share verbally or add sticky note responses to a shared bulletin board.

8. For most of the remainder of the class, students will practice the two-string practice options at their own pace, alone or with peers. Circle around the room and check in with each of them. Start with any students that did not follow along with the warmup. Support students as needed, by tracking the music with a pencil or finger, demonstrating fingerings, breaking down sections of the music, or providing auditory examples. Offer audio recordings or examples via notation software that students can refer to if auditory learning is their access point. Different options for visual representation should be available as well (see below).

9. At the end of class, check in with students before they pack up. Ask each student to find a note (B–G) on the first or second string and either tell you the position of the note or show it to you on their guitar as their "exit ticket" to pack up.

Materials:

1. Guitars. Students may benefit from the following accommodations:

    ○ color coding on frets with colored vinyl strips (beneficial for students with visual or working memory impairment; see Figures 6.1 and 6.2)

- smaller guitar sizes, or use of baritone ukulele, if available (beneficial for students with smaller body sizes or motor skill impairment)
- virtual guitars (beneficial for students with physical disabilities and/or fine motor skill impairment)
- nylon strings versus steel strings, or the use of a glove on the fretting hand (beneficial for students with hypersensitivity to touch or pressure)

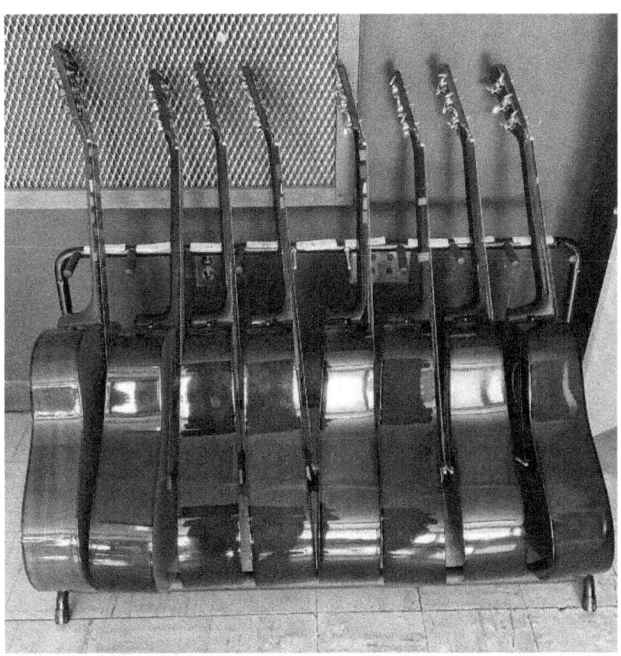

Figure 6.1. Colored vinyl is affixed to the fretboards of some guitars. Color-coded guitars are part of the classroom inventory, destigmatizing the adaptation.

Figure 6.2. Colored vinyl on the fretboard of a guitar. Numbers can also be added to the colored strips. Frets are colored as follows: orange (1), blue (2), yellow (3), green (4), red (5), lavender (6), brown (7), pink (8).

2. Music literacy materials (handouts) and auditory examples. Handouts should be available in a variety of formats, such as:
   - "La Bamba" black and white staff notation (Figure 6.3)
   - "La Bamba" color-coded staff notation (color coded by fret to reinforce finger position or fret position) with pitch names inside noteheads (Figure 6.4)
   - "La Bamba" color-coded tab notation (color coded by fret) (Figure 6.5)
   - "La Bamba" color-adapted tab block notation (Figure 6.6)
   - "Ode to Joy" black and white staff notation (Figure 6.7)
   - "Ode to Joy" color-coded staff notation (color coded by fret to reinforce finger position or fret position) with pitch names inside noteheads (Figure 6.8)
   - "Ode to Joy" color-coded tab notation (color coded by fret) (Figure 6.9)
   - "Ode to Joy" color-adapted tab block notation (Figure 6.10)
3. Other possible materials: Guitar picks and guitar straps. Autoharp or thumb picks can also be beneficial for students who benefit from the use of a pick but have difficulty holding onto one.

La Bamba

Traditional

Figure 6.3. "La Bamba" option 1, staff notation, black and white

La Bamba

Traditional

Figure 6.4. "La Bamba" option 2, color-coded staff notation with pitch names inside. All first fret notes (C and F) are colored orange. Third fret notes (D) are colored yellow. Open strings are left black.

La Bamba

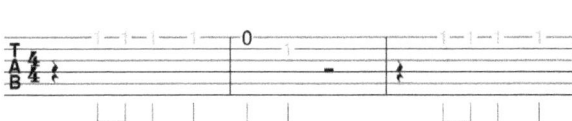

Figure 6.5. "La Bamba" option 3, color-coded tab notation. All first fret notes (C and F) are colored orange. Third fret notes (D) are colored yellow. Open strings are left black.

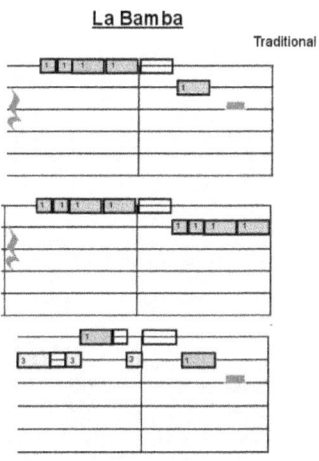

Figure 6.6. "La Bamba" option 4, color block tab notation. Colored blocks on tab lines correspond with fretboard colors for finger placement, with numbers for added support. All first fret notes (C and F) are colored orange. Third fret notes (D) are colored yellow. Open string blocks are left empty.

Ode To Joy

Beethoven

Figure 6.7. "Ode to Joy" option 1, staff notation, black and white

Ode To Joy

Beethoven

Figure 6.8. "Ode to Joy" option 2, color-coded staff notation. All first fret notes (C and F) are colored orange. Third fret notes (D and G) are colored yellow. Open strings are left black.

SAMPLE LESSONS

Ode To Joy

Beethoven

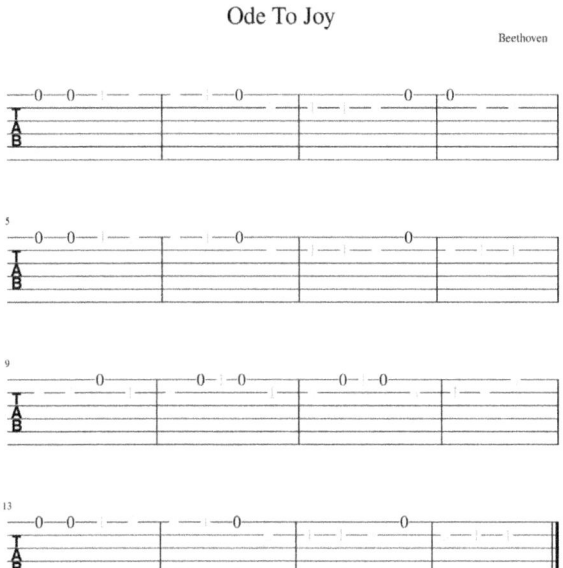

Figure 6.9. "Ode to Joy" option 3, color-coded tab notation. All first fret notes (C and F) are colored orange. Third fret notes (D and G) are colored yellow. Open strings are left black.

Figure 6.10. "Ode to Joy" option 4, color block tab notation. Colored blocks on tab lines correspond with fretboard colors for finger placement, with numbers for added support. All first fret notes (C and F) are colored orange. Third fret notes (D and G) are colored yellow. Open string blocks are left empty.

Assessment: Students should be given a rubric before the assessment. The rubric should be generalized and not specific to posture, tempo, or fingerings. This way, students with different physical abilities and processing speeds can use the same rubric. Individual goalposts (fingerings, tempo) should be determined by the student. Allow time for feedback, reflection, and discussion with students when presentation of their selected piece is assessed.

Music assessment is often very performance-driven, and performance anxiety is a real thing! If you teach general music electives that students do not necessarily sign up for, like I do, I suggest avoiding situations where students are required to perform for their peers. Instead, approach assessment as a way to allow students to demonstrate their knowledge and build skills toward overcoming performance anxiety. Options for how students can demonstrate their ability to present their selected piece include:

- one on one, during independent practice time
- via a recording that the teacher can review and both the student and the teacher can give feedback on
- via a screen recording if the student is using a virtual instrument and presenting asynchronously
- demonstrating fretting without playing the guitar

Sample Lesson: Elementary General Music

Grade level/ensemble: 3 or 4, general music (recorder)

Objectives: Students will be able to demonstrate the ability to play short pieces using B, A, and G on the recorder and create their own pattern using B, A, and G.

Number of classes for lesson: Two to four

Background information needed for this lesson: Students should already have experience using B, A, and G in practice, as well as rhythmic practice on quarter, half, and eighth note patterns.

NCAS: The following anchor standards are addressed:

- Anchor Standard 4: Select, analyze, and interpret artistic work for presentation.
- Anchor Standard 6: Convey meaning through the presentation of artistic work.
- Anchor Standard 7: Perceive and analyze artistic work.
- Anchor Standard 1: Generate and conceptualize artistic ideas and work.
- Anchor Standard 2: Organize and develop artistic ideas and work.

Procedure:

1. Begin with a warmup of quarter and eighth note rhythms. Use visuals of standard rhythm notation, with blocks underneath the rhythm symbols to denote duration. Ask students for words of one and two syllables. Write corresponding words into the empty blocks.

2. Keep a steady beat with a metronome or percussion instrument while having students chant the words

in time. Then, add body percussion. Students have the choice to clap, tap, or stomp. Modify this step by allowing students to demonstrate with only physical or vocal participation.

3. Next, prompt the students to take out their recorders without assembling them. Ask students how to play a B on their recorder. Students might answer verbally or show this on the body of the recorder. Then, prompt to students to assemble their recorders.

4. Count the students in to play the rhythm on a B note. Assess during this time who might need extra support. As students play the exercise, model the fingering while chanting the rhythm syllables.

5. Do the same exercise for A and G. G is a newer note, so it may need more review.

6. Place students in groups and instruct them to determine a pattern of B, A, and G notes by assigning each note of the rhythm warmup a letter. Give students the option of using graphic organizers or manipulatives. Set a visual timer for 5 to 10 minutes and, once the time is up, ask students to share their ideas. Students can present by playing their recorders or having the teacher play their written pattern.

7. Signal students to take the head joints off of their recorders and watch/listen to "Hot Cross Buns" and "Mary Had a Little Lamb." Explain that they will practice the fingerings for the two songs independently.

8. Allow time for individual or group work in practicing the fingerings along with reading the rhythms of both songs. Use this time to assess students in small groups. Give checklists to students who need extra

executive functioning support. If students are able to demonstrate fingerings, have them add their head joint and work through playing the songs with you. Assess who may need help with tonguing, blowing into the mouthpiece appropriately, and other required skills. Encourage students who have checked in with you to move forward in their practice.

9. Once you've checked in with all students, bring the group back together to play through both practice pieces. Use various tempos and genres of backing track music. Pause after each run through and ask for feedback (thumbs up, sideways, or down). Demonstrate fingerings as the students play, while also singing the note names. Be ready to track the music for anyone that might need it. The first few days, be sure to break the songs into sections during group rehearsal.

10. Offer opportunities for any student(s) who would like to do so to demonstrate one of the selections to the class. During the two to four days spent on this unit, give students the opportunity to tell you when they are ready to present their choice of either song for assessment.

11. At the end of the class, ask students to show you one of the notes (B, A, or G) as an exit ticket to pack up.

Materials:

1. Recorders. Students may benefit from the following accommodations:
   - color coding on finger holes with reinforcers (visual or working memory impairment; see Figure 6.11)

- keeping the recorder in their lap and simply focusing on fingering for the entirety of the lesson, if they do not have the coordination or hand strength developed yet

- virtual recorders (beneficial for students with physical disabilities and/or fine motor skill impairment)

- an adapted recorder, such as the Nuvo Recorder+

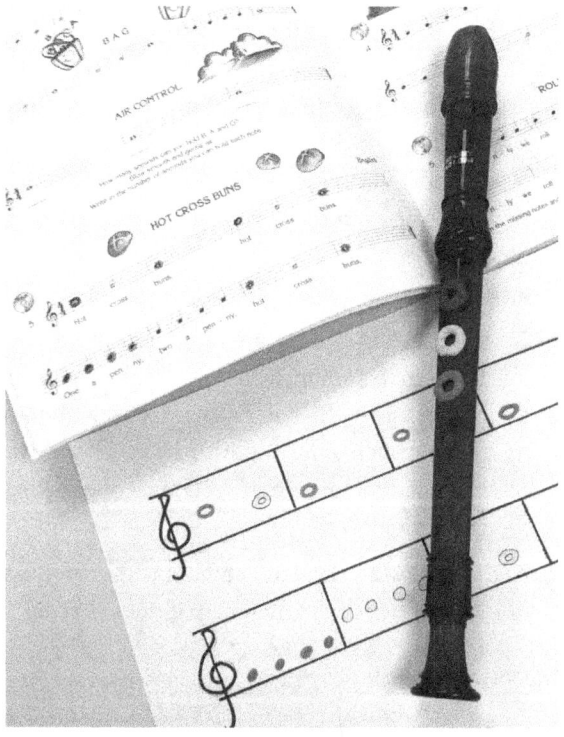

Figure 6.11. Colors, corresponding with the colors of the notation, are added to the finger holes of the recorder. This can be done with silicone rubber (pictured), stickers, or any other material that adds texture and color to the instrument.

2. Music literacy materials (handouts) and auditory examples. Handouts should be available in a variety of formats, such as:
   - "Hot Cross Buns" color-coded block notation with pitch names inside (Figure 6.12)
   - "Hot Cross Buns" color-coded rhythmic notation with pitch names inside (Figure 6.13)
   - "Hot Cross Buns" color-coded staff notation with pitch names inside (Figure 6.14)
   - "Hot Cross Buns" staff notation (Figure 6.15)
   - "Mary Had a Little Lamb" color-coded block notation with pitch names inside (Figure 6.16)
   - "Mary Had a Little Lamb" color-coded rhythmic notation with pitch names inside (Figure 6.17)
   - "Mary Had a Little Lamb" color-coded staff notation with pitch names inside (Figure 6.18)
   - "Mary Had a Little Lamb" staff notation (Figure 6.19)
3. Other possible materials: Mirrors on music stands so that students can better see their fingerings or mouth on the mouthpiece.

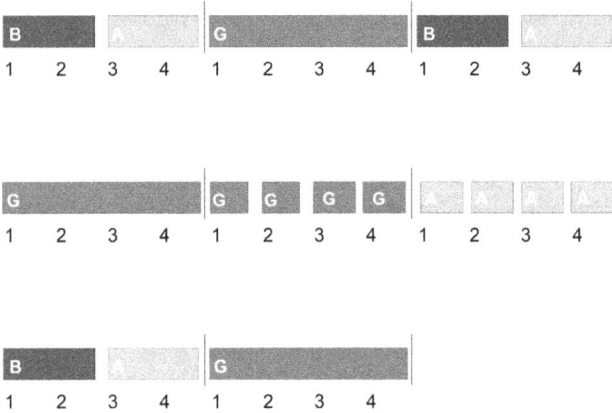

Figure 6.12. "Hot Cross Buns" option 1, color-coded block notation with pitch names inside. B is blue, A is yellow, and G is red.

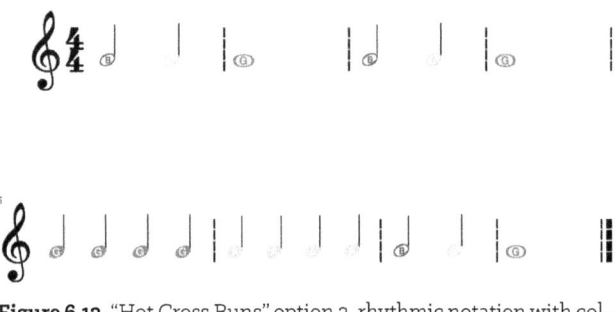

Figure 6.13. "Hot Cross Buns" option 2, rhythmic notation with colors and pitch names. B is blue, A is yellow, and G is red.

Figure 6.14. "Hot Cross Buns" option 3, staff notation with colors and pitch names. B is blue, A is yellow, and G is red.

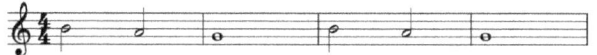

Figure 6.15. "Hot Cross Buns" option 4, staff notation, black and white

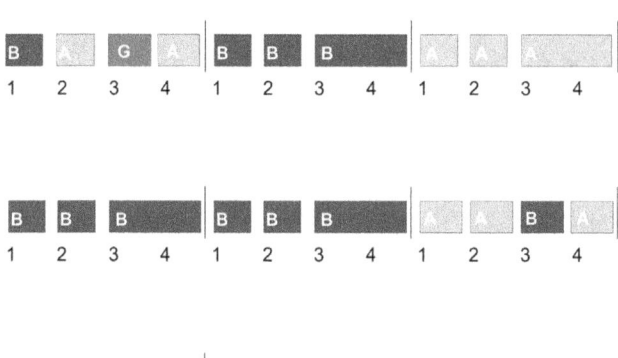

Figure 6.16. "Mary Had a Little Lamb" option 1, color-coded block notation with pitch names inside. B is blue, A is yellow, and G is red.

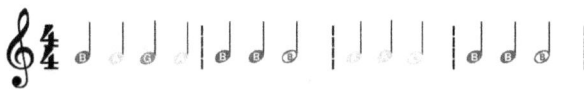

Figure 6.17. "Mary Had a Little Lamb" option 2, rhythmic notation with colors and pitch names. B is blue, A is yellow, and G is red.

Figure 6.18. "Mary Had a Little Lamb" option 3, staff notation with colors and pitch names. B is blue, A is yellow, and G is red.

Figure 6.19. "Mary Had a Little Lamb" option 4, staff notation, black and white

Assessment: Students will use a rubric that the class created at the beginning of the recorder unit. When students offer to demonstrate their chosen selection for assessment, review the rubric with them pre- and post-presentation and grade the presentation with them. This assessment can be modified by allowing students to demonstrate fingering without blowing into the instrument, or with a graphic organizer in which students fill in a fingering chart for each pitch of their selection. Students should be offered the choice of an in-person or video presentation.

Sample Lesson: High School Jazz Band

Grade level/ensemble: High school jazz band. The following lesson plan materials can be applied to a variety of beginner/intermediate Bossa Nova charts.

Objectives: Students will be able to recognize a Bossa Nova groove and be able to play through an example selection in time together. The supplemental materials in this example will focus on the drum set part.

Number of classes for lesson: One

Background information needed for this lesson: Students have not yet played a Bossa Nova tune this year.

NCAS: The following anchor standards are addressed:

- Anchor Standard 6: Convey meaning through the presentation of artistic work.
- Anchor Standard 7: Perceive and analyze artistic work.
- Anchor Standard 1: Generate and conceptualize artistic ideas and work.
- Anchor Standard 2: Organize and develop artistic ideas and work.

Procedure:

1. Play a selected Bossa Nova song as students walk into class.
2. Display a color/shape-coded basic Bossa Nova drum set pattern on the board. Colors and shapes (green X, red circle, blue X within a box) can correlate to labels on the drum set for students who benefit from supports. If there is room, include

MIDI notation as well, or another graphic form of notation, underneath the standard notation (Figure 6.20).

3. Encourage students to try the kick, snare, and hi-hat patterns on their own before the class tries it together. Students who excel at the rhythms have the option of trying two or more together with body percussion. Use this time to assess who might need extra support with the rhythm. Have mini-whiteboards or worksheets ready for students who benefit from having the pattern on their music stand, with opportunities for writing in counting or other supportive text.

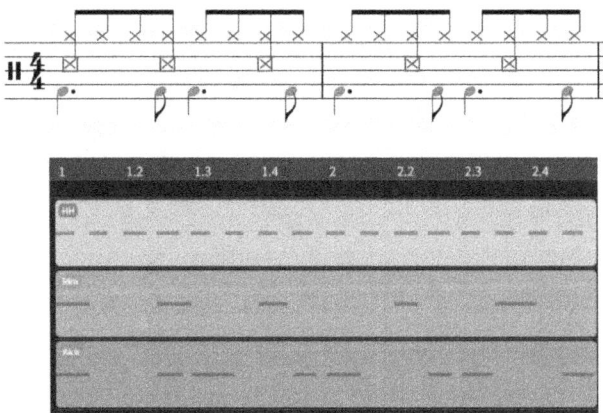

Figure 6.20. A color-coded display of the Bossa Nova drum set pattern allows for parts of the drum set to be annotated with colors and shapes to correspond to the notation. In this example, a MIDI visual is displayed below the Western standard staff notation, with matching colors.

4. Get the class's attention and pause the music. Ask if anyone has heard the song before. Students can reply with a nonverbal gesture (thumbs up or down) or verbally. Ask for a few volunteers to share where they have heard it.

5. Explain where Brazil is, showing it on a map if possible. Share with the class that Bossa Nova originated in Brazil. Encourage students to do a little research and be ready to share any facts they learn about Bossa Nova in the next class. Students will be able to share vocally or by adding notes to a shared idea board (which can be physical or digital).

6. Bring the class's attention to the rhythm on the board that they have been practicing. Review the counting of the pattern, writing the counts underneath the rhythm symbols and circling the beats (and half beats) to be played on. Play the pattern for them.

7. Start a metronome at a medium tempo and have the class say and/or clap the rhythm of the kick drum. Encourage the drummer to play the rhythm on the kick drum. Then, add the hi-hat pattern. Students can choose to stay on the kick or clap/say the hi-hat. Lastly, add the snare pattern, using the same approach to dividing the class.

8. Next, give the class a few moments (use of a timer is encouraged for transparency) to independently review their concert pitch F major scale. Students should have visual materials accessible to them to support recall of fingerings if needed. The drummer should use this time to put the Bossa Nova pattern together.

9. Bring the class back together and demonstrate playing the scale over the Bossa Nova rhythm. Ask a volunteer to demonstrate the same thing.

10. Have the drummer start the Bossa Nova pattern and then count the class in to play the scale forward and backward, four beats per note. Do this a few times at different tempos, each time pausing at the end for student feedback (verbal and nonverbal).

11. Next, demonstrate the A section of the selected chart with the drummer playing the Bossa Nova beat. Demonstrate each instrument's part if time allows, or the lead if time is short. Then, play a recorded example of how everything will sound together. Divide students into sectionals to review the A section. Encourage students who excel in sectionals to move on to the B section.

12. Use the time in sectionals to assess who needs more support in tracking, decoding, and so forth. Auditory references should be made available to students during this time; this will be beneficial for those that have strength in auditory learning.

13. At the end of class, bring all the sectionals back together and practice the A section as a group.

Materials:

1. Instruments. Students may benefit from the following accommodations:
   - color coding/shape coding/numbers on finger holes (if applicable), slide positions, drum set parts, or keys/frets that correspond with the notation

- color coding to indicate octaves on the piano and/or octave keys that correspond with the notation
- fingering/fretting notes without blowing/buzzing
- virtual instruments
- adapted instruments, such as NUVO instruments

2. Music literacy materials (handouts) and auditory examples. Handouts should be available in a variety of formats, including modified parts. Possible formats (depending on instrumentation) include:
   - color-coded block notation with labels inside (Figure 6.21)
   - color-coded rhythmic notation with labels inside (Figure 6.22)
   - color-coded rhythmic notation with pitch names inside, modified part (Figure 6.23)
   - color-coded staff notation with note names inside (Figure 6.24)
   - color-coded staff notation with note names inside, modified part (Figure 6.25)
   - staff notation (Figure 6.26)
   - staff notation, modified part (Figure 6.27)
   - tablature
   - color-coded tablature
   - chord charts
   - color-coded chord charts

Color coding can refer to fingerings/instrument parts, or if an octave key is needed. Labels can refer to pitch name or instrument, in the case of drum set.

3. Other possible materials: Mirrors on music stands so that students can better see their fingerings or mouth on the mouthpiece, grips added to drumsticks, headphones for students who are sensitive to sound.

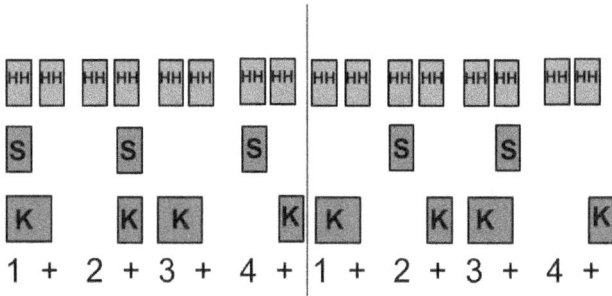

Figure 6.21. A basic Bossa Nova pattern for drum set is displayed in color-coded block notation, where half blocks represent eighth notes and full blocks represent one beat. The kick drum (K) is red, snare drum (S) is blue, and hi-hat (HH) is green. These colors should correlate with color labels on the drum set parts.

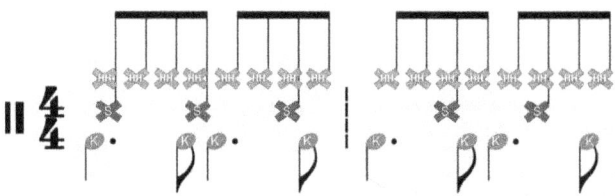

Figure 6.22. A basic Bossa Nova pattern for drum set is displayed in color-coded standard rhythm notation. The kick drum (K) is red, snare drum (S) is blue, and hi-hat (HH) is green. These colors should correlate with color labels on the drum set parts.

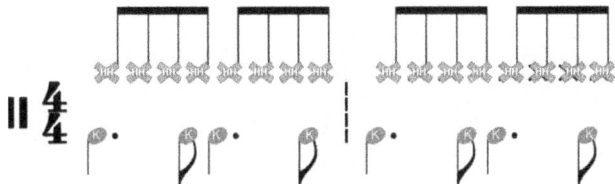

Figure 6.23. A modified Bossa Nova pattern for drum set is displayed in color-coded standard rhythm notation, omitting the snare drum portion of the pattern. The kick drum (K) is red and hi-hat (HH) is green. These colors should correlate with color labels on the drum set parts.

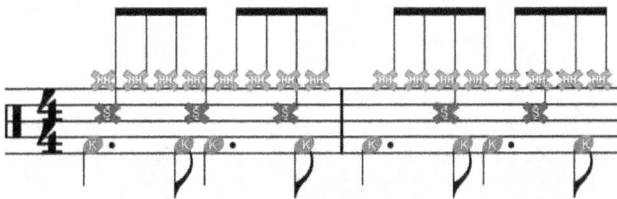

Figure 6.24. A basic Bossa Nova pattern for drum set is displayed in color-coded standard staff notation. Letters and colors are still available for supports: the kick drum (K) is red, snare drum (S) is blue, and hi-hat (HH) is green. These colors should correlate with color labels on the drum set parts. This option can be helpful for students who benefit from supports but want to transition to reading standard notation.

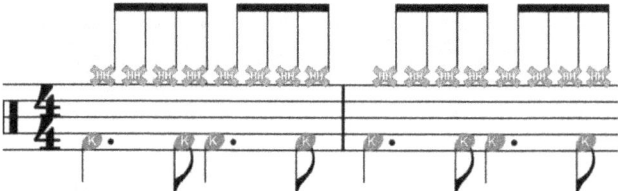

Figure 6.25. A modified Bossa Nova pattern for drum set is displayed in color-coded standard staff notation, omitting the snare drum portion of the pattern. Letters and colors are still available for supports: the kick drum (K) is red and hi-hat (HH) is green. These colors should correlate with color labels on the drum set parts. This option can be helpful for students who benefit from supports but want to transition to reading standard notation.

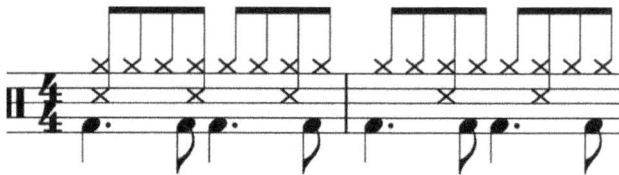

Figure 6.26. A basic Bossa Nova pattern for drum set is displayed in standard staff notation.

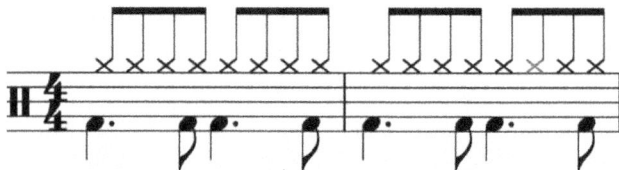

Figure 6.27. A modified Bossa Nova pattern for drum set is displayed in standard staff notation, omitting the snare drum portion of the pattern.

Assessment: Assessment for an activity such as this is formative. Using a checklist with your attendance sheet can be helpful for keeping track of who needs more or less support during sectional practice and warmups. Students are able to demonstrate their knowledge through speaking or clapping the rhythm patterns, demonstrating fingerings in various tempos, or playing the pitch and rhythm together.

References

Hammel, A. M., & Hourigan, R. M. (2013). *Teaching music to students with autism*. Oxford University Press.

Lesiuk, T. (2015). Music perception ability of children with executive function deficits. *Psychology of Music, 43*(4), 530–544.

McKoy, C. L., & Lind, V. R. (2016). *Culturally responsive teaching in music education: From understanding to application*. Routledge.

Meyer, A., Rose, D., & Gordon, D. (2024). *Universal Design for Learning: Principles, framework, and practice*. CAST Professional Publishing.

Miller, J. R. (2016). Creating choirs that welcome transgender singers. *Choral Journal, 57*(4), 61–63. https://www.jstor.org/stable/24883861

Overy, K., Nicolson, R. I., Fawcett, A. J., & Clarke, E. F. (2003). Dyslexia and music: Measuring musical timing skills. *Dyslexia, 9*(1), 18–36. https://doi.org/10.1002/dys.233

Tan, S.-L., Wakefield, E. M., & Jeffries, P. W. (2009). Musically untrained college students' interpretations of musical notation: Sound, silence, loudness, duration, and temporal order. *Psychology of Music, 37*(1), 5–24. https://doi.org/10.1177/0305735608090845

Wehr, E. L. (2015). Understanding the experiences of women in jazz: A suggested model. *International Journal of Music Education, 34*(4), 472–487.

Wiggins, G., & McTighe, J. (2005). *Understanding by design* (2nd ed.). Association for Supervision and Curriculum Development.

CAST Skinny Books®

"Don't tell me everything. Just give me the skinny!"™

CAST Professional Publishing produces books that help educators at all levels improve their practice—and change students' lives—through Universal Design for Learning (UDL). We create, nurture, and distribute exceptional media products that inspire and inform educational research, instructional practice, and policy making for the betterment of all.

Skinny Books by CAST address critical topics of education practice through brief, informative publications that emphasize practical tips and strategies. We talk about these books as "multivitamins"—densely packed with helpful knowledge in a small, digestible format.

We welcome new proposals. Got an idea? Let us know at *publishing@cast.org*.

While every Skinny Book will be in tune with the inclusive principles of Universal Design for Learning, not every title needs to address UDL specifically. For those that do, the authors may assume readers have a knowledge of UDL already, as we've done in *Art for All*.

If you need an introduction to UDL, visit *udlguidelines.cast.org*.

You can also purchase this or many other titles on UDL from *www.castpublishing.org*.

MORE FROM CAST

CAST is a nonprofit education research and development organization that created the Universal Design for Learning framework and UDL Guidelines. Our mission is to transform education design and practice until learning has no limits.

CAST supports learners and educators at every level through a variety of offerings:

- Innovative professional development
- Accessibility and inclusive technology resources
- Research, design, and development of inclusive and effective solutions
- Credentials for Universal Design for Learning
- And much more

Visit *www.cast.org* to learn more.

www.ingramcontent.com/pod-product-compliance
Lightning Source LLC
Chambersburg PA
CBHW050039080526
44586CB00014B/1379